SPOTLIGHT
ON CHILDREN'S
AUTHORS

MAURICE SENDAK

WENDY MEAD

Cavendish
Square

New York

Published in 2015 by Cavendish Square Publishing, LLC
303 Park Avenue South, Suite 1247, New York, NY 10010

Website: cavendishsq.com

This publication represents the opinions and views of the author based on his or her personal experience, knowledge, and research. The information in this book serves as a general guide only. The author and publisher have used their best efforts in preparing this book and disclaim liability rising directly or indirectly from the use and application of this book.

CPSIA Compliance Information: Batch #WS14CSQ

All websites were available and accurate when this book was sent to press.

Library of Congress Cataloging-in-Publication Data
Mead, Wendy.
Maurice Sendak / Wendy Mead.
pages cm — (Spotlight on children's authors)
Includes bibliographical references and index.
ISBN 978-1-62712-840-7 (hardcover) ISBN 978-1-62712-841-4 (paperback) ISBN 978-1-62712-842-1 (ebook)
1. Sendak, Maurice—Juvenile literature. 2. Authors, American—20th century—Biography—Juvenile literature. 3. Children's literature—Authorship—Juvenile literature. 4. Illustrators—United States—Biography—Juvenile literature. I. Title.

PS3569.E6Z766 2014
813'.54—dc23
[B]

2013050652

Editorial Director: Dean Miller
Editor: Andrew Coddington
Senior Copy Editor: Wendy A. Reynolds
Art Director: Jeffrey Talbot
Designer: Amy Greenan
Production Manager: Jennifer Ryder-Talbot
Production Editor: David McNamara
Photo Research: J8 Media

The photographs in this book with permission and through courtesy of: cover courtesy of James Keyser/Time & Life Images/Getty Images; AP Photo/Thomas Victor, 4; MBR/KRT/Newscom, 5; AP Photo/General Motors Corp., 6; Walt Disney/Mary Evans Picture Library Ltd/age fotostock, 11; Spencer Platt/Getty Images, 12; AL FENN/Time & Life Pictures/Getty Images, 16; AP Photo, 18; Hulton Archive/Getty Images, 20; AP Photo/HarperCollins, copyright © 1970 by Maurice Sendak, 22; AP Photo/Francesco Guazzeli, Syracuse University in Florence, 24; ©Guy Gravett Collection/ArenaPAL/The Image Works, 27; Bloomberg/Getty Images, 28; NY Daily News/Getty Images, 30; Keystone/Hulton Archive/Getty Images, 33; Theo Wargo/WireImage/Getty Images, 34; Ronald Grant/Mary Evans Picture Library Ltd/age fotostock, 36; AP Photo/HarperCollins, copyright © 2011 by Maurice Sendak, 38.

Printed in the United States of America

CONTENTS

Maurice Sendak helped change the world of children's books by creating imaginative stories that touched on real fantasies and fears of the young. With *Where the Wild Things Are*, he took readers on an exciting yet scary journey.

Max, the book's main character, fights with his mother and is sent to his room without dinner. A short time later, he travels to a faraway land filled with strange creatures. He manages to tame these wild things by looking them in the eye and showing no fear. In the end, however, Max is drawn back to his everyday life by the smells of home.

When this book was published in 1963, many adults didn't know what to make of it. Some found the story too scary for children. Others thought the illustrations were strange and dark. Despite these criticisms, *Where the Wild Things Are* proved to be a groundbreaking book. Sendak brought to the page tales filled with real childhood experiences.

Sendak won the Caldecott Award for *Where the Wild Things Are* the following year. In his acceptance speech for this honor, he talked about how children use imaginative play to conquer the challenges they face in their everyday lives. "Max, the hero of my book, discharges his anger against his mother and returns to the real world sleepy, hungry, and at peace with himself."

Since its publication, *Where the Wild Things Are* has captured the imagination of generations of kids. It has sold more than ten million copies, and has been translated into at least sixteen languages. *Where the Wild Things Are* has also been made into an opera and a full-length movie.

Throughout his career, Sendak valued honesty in his work. He showed children as they really were. His characters get mad, fight with their parents, and boss their friends around. These children also prove to be heroes in their own way. They face their fears and overcome many dangerous situations. Sendak felt it was important to be candid about the world with his readers. As he explained on the *Fresh Air* radio program, "I've convinced myself ... that children despair of you if you don't tell them the truth."

One of Maurice's favorite childhood memories was of visiting the 1939 World's Fair with his older brother Jack.

Chapter 1
GROWING UP IN BROOKLYN

Born on June 10, 1928, **Maurice Bernard Sendak** was the youngest of three children. He lived in Brooklyn with his parents Philip and Sarah, who was called "Sadie." His sister, Natalie, was eleven years older than he was, and brother, Jack, was five years older. Known as "Murray" or "Moishe" growing up, he was closer to his siblings than he was to his parents. "I felt more parent affection coming from my brother and sister," he told the *New Yorker* magazine. "I was very lucky to have two siblings of opposite sexes, so I could have another mother and another father and ones I really adored."

While he lived in America, Sendak's early life was steeped in the customs and traditions of the "Old Country." His parents were both Jewish immigrants who came to the United States from Poland. The couple met and married once they arrived in their new home country. Philip, a tailor, had left Poland in search of a better life. He was eventually able to start his own business. However, not long after Maurice arrived, Philip had to close his garment factory. In 1929, the United States plunged into the Great Depression with the crash of the American stock market. Millions of people lost their money when the stocks they owned lost their value. Companies were also wiped out, losing the money they needed to run their businesses.

As the country struggled financially, young Maurice Sendak encountered his own troubles. He was a sickly child, spending much of his time inside. His parents worried about his health. They even told him that he might die. Sendak had a number of illnesses, including measles, scarlet fever, and pneumonia, all of which were considered deadly at the time. Still, he managed to survive, and to put his time stuck in bed to good use. Sendak developed a passion for reading and drawing—both quiet activities he could do safely tucked away in his room.

It was not just his health that worried Sendak. Some of the events going on around him scared him as well. He had been frightened by stories about the kidnapping of the son of a famous pilot, Charles Lindbergh. The baby boy was taken from the Lindberghs' home in New Jersey in March 1932. Even though the Lindbergh family tried to pay the ransom the kidnappers demanded, the baby was found dead two months later. Sendak felt that if a wealthy, well-known family couldn't keep their child safe, no one could. The notion of stolen children cropped up later in his books. Maurice's own father didn't help dispel his fears much, either. Philip Sendak had a habit of telling his children disturbing bedtime stories.

Sendak also grew up in a time of great wonder. He loved visiting the New York World's Fair in 1939. Spread across more than 1,200 acres in Queens, New York, the theme of the event was "The World

COMING TO AMERICA

Philip Sendak left his native Poland for love. A young woman he was dating moved to the United States. In July 1913, Philip arrived in New York after traveling across the ocean on a ship called the *President Grant*. But he soon learned his sweetheart had already married someone else. Philip later met Sarah at a wedding.

of Tomorrow," and its exhibits offered visitors a view of the future. There were also rides and shows as well. The fair left such an impression on Sendak and his brother, Jack, that they built a model of it out of wax. This was just one of many projects that the Sendak brothers did together. From the very beginning of Maurice's life, Jack served as a companion, teacher, and friend. "He took his time with me to draw pictures and to read stories and live a fantastical life," Sendak told the radio program *Fresh Air*.

Around the age of nine, Sendak started working on stories with his brother. Jack wrote the words, and Maurice made the pictures to go with it. One of their stories was called "They Were Inseparable." It was about a brother and sister who fall in love with each other. The pair meets a tragic end.

Going to the movies was another activity that Sendak loved as a child. He would go to the theater with his siblings to see the latest films. He loved comedies with Charlie Chaplin, Stan Laurel, and Oliver Hardy. The 1933 action adventure tale *King Kong* also left a lasting impression on Sendak. The film showed a giant ape running wild in New York City. But the character that meant the most to him was Mickey Mouse. For the rest of his life, he continued to be fascinated by this cartoon mouse.

Sendak hated school growing up. He was left-handed, but his teachers would force him to use his right. He much preferred to sit by the window in his apartment. Always fond of drawing, Sendak liked to record what he saw in the street outside his window. He would sit for hours, sketching the activities of his neighbors. A young girl named Rosie was featured in some of these drawings. Sendak was fascinated by the plays Rosie performed with her friends. Many years later, he used the girl from his neighborhood as the inspiration for one of his books.

World events continued to cast a dark shadow over Sendak's early life. He was a teenager during World War II. Sendak's family suffered many personal losses during this time. His sister's fiancé was killed while serving in the military. His brother Jack was also a soldier. Jack was missing in action for a while in the Philippines in 1944. Luckily, he managed to return home safely. Other members of the family weren't so lucky, unfortunately. Sendak's father learned that some of his family had been killed when German forces invaded their village in Poland in 1941. Those who did survive the attack were sent off to concentration camps where they eventually perished. During the war, both of his parents grieved for the family members they lost to the German persecution of the Jews.

MICKEY MOUSE

Maurice Sendak was born in the same year as the cartoon character Mickey Mouse. Mickey Mouse first graced film screens across the country in 1928 in "Steamboat Willie." Walt Disney created Mickey Mouse and he even did the character's voice in some of the early cartoons. During his lifetime, Sendak developed one of the largest collections of Mickey Mouse-related items. But he only liked things that showed Mickey in his early years, nothing past 1940.

Despite these difficult times, Sendak began to thrive as an artist. He wrote a comic strip for the Lafayette High School newspaper. He was so talented that he landed a job with All-American Comics. After school, Sendak would work on the backgrounds for *Mutt and Jeff*. *Mutt and Jeff* was created by Bud Fisher in 1907. It was one of the first successful daily newspaper comic strips.

Sendak worked at the famous toy store FAO Schwarz, making window displays like the one shown here.

Chapter 2
SENDAK'S EARLY CAREER

While still in high school, Sendak landed his first job as a book illustrator. His physics teacher gave him the task of drawing pictures for a book he co-wrote titled *Atomics for the Millions*, published in 1947. Sendak was paid $100 for his artwork. Some reports indicate these sketches also helped improve his less-than-great grade in physics as well.

After graduation, Sendak put his artistic talents to a new use. He went to work for a Manhattan company called Timely Service. There he worked on making window displays for stores. His projects included creating papier mâché sculptures of the characters from Snow White.

"It was one of the best times of my life," Sendak later said in Selma G. Lanes' *The Art of Maurice Sendak*. "I was meeting all kinds of people I'd never met in Brooklyn. They were people who felt that they were really artists and considered their work." Like his coworkers, Sendak focused on his own art in his spare time. He took some classes at the Art Students League of New York.

Working with his brother, Jack, Sendak started making toys. Jack handled the design and carving of these wooden pieces, and Maurice did the painting. Some of their toys showed scenes from fairy tales. One had Little Red Riding Hood standing by her grandmother's bedside. With a pull of a lever, the wolf popped up, and Little Red Riding Hood fell down. The Sendak brothers took their creations to the famous New York toy store FAO Schwartz.

While the store wasn't interested in the toys, Maurice Sendak did end up getting a job there. He worked as a window dresser, helping to create displays for the store. Sendak befriended the children's book buyer for the store. She, in turn, introduced him to legendary children's book editor Ursula Nordstrom.

Nordstrom was the head of the children's book department of Harper and Brothers, which is now known as HarperCollins. She visited Sendak in his work space at FAO Schwartz where she saw some of his early sketches. With her help, Sendak landed one of his first assignments as an illustrator. His first published project, *The Wonderful Farm* by Marcel Ayme, was released in 1951.

Sendak collaborated with author Ruth Krauss on several titles, starting with 1952's *A Hole Is to Dig*—an unusual book for its time. Rather than follow a traditional storyline, the book was a collection of children's definitions of commonplace things. Sendak spent weekends with Krauss and her husband, Crockett Johnson, at their house in Connecticut. Johnson was the creator of the *Barnaby* comic strip and a children's book illustrator himself.

In an article for *The Horn Book* Magazine, Sendak wrote that *A Hole Is to Dig* was "my official baptism into picture books." He credited Krauss and Crockett with "shaping me into an artist." Sendak told the *Los Angeles Times* that Crockett gave him reading lists to help him broaden his knowledge. Since he never went to college, he considered his time with them to be his own special kind of education.

Delving deeper into the world of children's books, Sendak illustrated several works by Meindert DeJong. He created the art for *Shadrach* (1953) and *The Wheel on the School* (1954) among other titles. Sendak also did a wonderful job illustrating Else Holmelund Minarik's popular *Little Bear* book series. Children's books were even a family affair for a time, since Maurice served as the illustrator on several books written by his own brother, Jack. *The Happy Rain* (1956) and *Circus Girl* (1957) were two of the titles the Sendak brothers did together.

With encouragement from Nordstrom, Sendak began work on his own books as well. His first effort at creating both the words and the pictures came together in 1956's *Kenny's Window*. Sendak used his childhood habit of watching out of his apartment window as part of the inspiration for this story. Like a young Sendak, the main character, Kenny, is often pictured gazing out his window. He is a boy alone in his room with only his imagination to keep him company. Sendak experienced this type of situation countless times growing up.

The story follows Kenny on an odd quest. He wants to live in a garden he has seen in his dreams. To accomplish this goal, he must

Much like the boy shown here, Sendak loved to watch the world from his apartment window. This habit inspired him to write *Kenny's Window*.

answer a series of seven questions. Kenny is helped along the way by animals and his own toys.

Sendak's stories also sprang from his Brooklyn neighborhood. *The Sign on Rosie's Door* (1960) featured a character much like the neighborhood girl named Rosie he spent so much time observing. His Rosie, like the original, acts as the director and producer of her own theatrical show. She pushes her friends into joining her and doing what she wants.

Sendak dedicated *The Sign on Rosie's Door* to a friend he made during the summer of 1944 while visiting the Berkshires with his family. Both he and Pearl Karchawer had brothers who were missing in action in the war. Sadly, Pearl died the following year after having surgery done on her back. Her unexpected death was yet another reminder of how fragile life really was.

In 1962, Sendak debuted his special collection of small books called The Nutshell Library. There were four titles: *Alligators All Around*, *Chicken Soup with Rice*, *One Was Johnny*, and *Pierre*. *Alligators All Around* is a fun romp through the alphabet, while *One Was Johnny* plays with numbers. *Chicken Soup with Rice* takes its readers through the calendar, depicting how this delightful dish fits in all seasons. Sendak dedicated this book to Mrs. Ida Perles, who was a second mother to him growing up. *Pierre* is billed as a cautionary tale. It follows the consequences a boy faces when he insists that he doesn't care about anything.

The Nutshell Library and *The Sign on Rosie's Door* later became the basis for a 1975 television special titled *Really Rosie*. Sendak worked with singer-songwriter Carole King to make this animated musical. On the program, King sings Sendak's words as the lyrics to the music she has written. The special was so popular that it was later turned into an off-Broadway show.

Sendak usually sketched out his images before making the artwork. Here he reviews a sketch while working on one of his characters.

Chapter 3
FAMOUS AUTHOR AND ILLUSTRATOR

By the early 1960s, Sendak was working steadily as an illustrator and author, but he really became famous with the publication of *Where the Wild Things Are* in 1963. Sendak's images in this story differed from the usual American children's book. The colors were deeper and richer than the bright and sunny style of other works for kids.

The way Sendak drew the character Max was also distinct. Like many of the children he drew over the years, Max has a roundish face and thick body. Sendak explained in *Tell Them Anything You Want*, a documentary about his work, that his pictures of kids came from his own experience. In most American children's books, the characters have "cute, upturned noses and a little puff of blond hair in the front." Those characters didn't look like the kids Sendak knew. Children he grew up with "all had squashed heads and thumpy, lumpy bodies."

Some of the book's characters drew inspiration from Sendak's life. Max's monsters were actually inspired by the relatives that made weekly visits to the Sendaks' home. He found these visits disturbing because his relatives really didn't know how to talk to him. Instead they often just pinched his cheeks too hard. Sendak also snuck in one of his favorite creatures into the book. He used his beloved dog Jennie as the model for the little dog Max chases in one illustration.

This adventurous tale of a boy who tames the wild things proved to be a big success. The book also earned him one of the top honors for children's book illustrators. In 1964, Sendak received the Caldecott Medal for *Where the Wild Things Are*. In his speech, he explained that the book "was not meant to please everybody— only children." Sendak went on to note that he had received a fan

THE MAN BEHIND THE MEDAL

The Caldecott Medal takes its name from English illustrator Randolph J. Caldecott. Caldecott was born on March 22, 1846, in Chester, England. He is best known for his illustrations of children's books during the 1800s. An admirer of Caldecott's work, Sendak loved his drawings for their sense of humor. He also liked how Caldecott was able to portray his figures in action. Sendak considered Caldecott to be the creator of the modern picture book for children.

letter from a young reader that asked, "How much does it cost to get to where the wild things are? If it's not too expensive my sister and I want to spend the summer there."

Oddly enough, it wasn't *Where the Wild Things Are* that won his father's approval. Philip Sendak was more impressed by Maurice's work illustrating *Nikolenka's Childhood* by Leo Tolstoy. According to *The Art of Maurice Sendak*, his father asked, "Does that mean they'll let you illustrate real books now?" His father's comment also showed the strained relationship between the two of them. Sendak never really got along with his parents.

A few years after the great success of *Where the Wild Things Are*, Sendak experienced a series of personal challenges. He traveled to England in May 1967 to meet with his English editor, Judy Taylor. Taylor worked for The Bodley Head publishing company. Sendak suffered a heart attack while doing a television interview. At first, he wasn't sure what was wrong and just wanted to rest. Luckily, Judy Taylor insisted he go to the hospital. He ended up at Queen Elizabeth Hospital in Gateshead-Upon-Tyne. For several weeks, Sendak stayed in the hospital recovering from this serious heart problem.

Upon his return, Sendak learned that his dog Jennie's health was failing. He had her put to sleep to end her suffering. A heartbroken Sendak had a chance to honor Jennie with the book *Higglety Pigglety Pop! Or There Must Be More to Life* (1967). Named for his beloved pet, a dog named Jennie decides to abandon her comfortable home for new adventures. She ends up becoming a successful actress in a theater company. In the end, Jennie writes a note to her former owner to say that she is never coming home.

Sendak again raised a few eyebrows with *In the Night Kitchen* (1970). This time around, some adults seemed uncomfortable with the main character Mickey's naked body in some of the illustrations. Some libraries even banned the book over these images. Others seemed bothered by the danger Mickey faced during the course of the story. At one point, he almost ends up being baked in a pie.

Yet *In the Night Kitchen* is a delight in many ways. Sendak used a different style for the book, giving it an almost comic-book feel. Mickey's story appears to be set in the 1930s. It serves as a tribute to Sendak's childhood. The three bakers Mickey encounters are all modeled on comedian Oliver Hardy of the famed Laurel and Hardy movies of the era. The setting of the kitchen also creates a feeling of warmth and comfort. Through *In the Night Kitchen*, readers get to tumble along with Mickey during his dream.

Around the time of *In the Night Kitchen*'s publication, Sendak received another major award—the Hans Christian Andersen International Medal. When he accepted this honor, Sendak explained that the goal of his work was to share his "Old Country-New Country childhood" through "words and pictures." He also made some changes in his personal life around this time, and decided to leave New York City. He sought out a new life in the country, buying a home in Ridgefield, Connecticut.

In 1981, Sendak published *Outside Over There*. This story follows Ida, who must rescue her baby sister from goblins. The goblins switched her sister for a baby made of ice when Ida wasn't looking. As in many Sendak stories, Ida must face danger head-on. She plays music on her horn to force the goblins to dance.

For the story, Sendak drew on many sources, especially the works of writers Jacob and Wilhelm Grimm, commonly known as the Brothers Grimm, and composer Wolfgang Amadeus Mozart. Another part of *Outside Over There* came from Sendak's own childhood fears. In the book, he touches on the Lindbergh baby kidnapping that haunted him in his youth. One of the drawings of the baby in the story is a portrait of the lost Lindbergh baby.

Outside Over There is considered to be the third title in a trilogy by Sendak. This set of books also includes *Where the Wild Things Are* and *In the Night Kitchen*. These three stories are linked because they tackle a similar idea: A child goes out on a journey, faces some challenges, and returns home safe.

For Sendak, *Outside Over There* proved to be a tremendous challenge. He later explained that he found the project so frustrating that he gave up on it. Remarkably, what saved both Sendak and the book was another creative opportunity. Frank Corsaro, a director of operas, called him to see if he wanted to work on a production with him.

Working on the opera Where the Wild Things Are
allowed Sendak to bring his characters to life
through set and costume design.

Chapter 4
CREATING ALL KINDS OF ART

Expanding beyond words and pictures on a page, Sendak tackled some theatrical challenges in the 1980s and 1990s. He began creating designs for stage sets and costumes. This new art form proved to be a life saver for him. Sendak first worked with Frank Corsaro on a 1980 production of *The Magic Flute* by Wolfgang Amadeus Mozart. As he explained to *The Horn Book Magazine*, this project had a wonderful healing effect on him: "I felt as if Mozart were the nurse taking care of me."

Juggling numerous projects at once, Sendak also worked on the stage production of *Really Rosie* around this same time. He also took on another opera—one based on material he was very familiar with. He collaborated with composer Oliver Knussen on his operatic take on *Where the Wild Things Are*. For this opera, Sendak wrote the libretto, or story, as well as designed the sets and costumes. Sendak worked with Knussen again as the composer translated *Higglety Pigglety Pop!* into an opera that premiered in 1984.

Sendak also continued to collaborate with Corsaro. Corsaro brought Sendak in to replace his original designer on a 1981 production of *The Cunning Little Vixen*. This opera by Leoš Janáčk follows the adventures of a female fox. The following year, Sendak saw another of his opera projects staged for the first time. He worked with Corsaro on the sets and costumes for *The Love for Three Oranges* by composer Sergey Prokofiev. The comedic opera was done for the Glyndebourne Festival in England.

One of his later projects with Corsaro revisited a classic fairy tale. They teamed up for a 1996 production of *Hansel and Gretel*, an opera by Engelbert Humperdinck. As he explained to *The New York Times*, this classical story teaches us "that children survive against all odds."

In addition to opera, Sendak used his creative energy on other works for the stage. He worked on the sets and costumes for the Pacific Northwest Ballet's *The Nutcracker* in 1983. This production was later turned into a film. He also formed a theater group for children called the Night Kitchen Theater Company with Arthur Yorinks. With this national theater group, Sendak worked on several shows. He created the sets and costumes for such plays as *It's Alive* (1994) and *Frank & Joey* (1995).

Sendak still worked on the occasional children's book project. It was around this time he finished the images for a very personal story. In 1970, while visiting Maurice, his father wrote a tale about the Old Country. This became the 1985 book *In Grandpa's House*. Delving into the past once more, Sendak did the illustrations for *Dear Mili* (1988). This is a deeply sad tale by Wilhelm Grimm that follows a young girl's search for her mother. It is one of the few books that Sendak worked on that does not have some type of happy ending.

Sendak also used his artistic talents for other types of work. A devoted reader of Herman Melville, he had a chance to illustrate one of Melville's works. Sendak made the images that accompanied a new edition of *Pierre; or, The Ambiguities* in 1995. For the project, he teamed up with Melville scholar Hershel

Sendak reviews part of a costume from the 1982 production of *The Love for Three Oranges.*

Parker. Parker thought the book would be better if certain chapters were cut out, and wanted to publish a new version of this 1852 novel. The revised book was called the "Kraken edition," named for an imaginary sea monster.

For much of his career, Sendak was frustrated by being labeled "a kiddie-book man," as he once told *Vanity Fair* magazine. He wanted to be taken seriously as an artist. Sendak got that wish in the late 1990s. In January 1997, he received the 1996 National Medal of Arts from President Bill Clinton. This honor put him in some very elite company. Other medal winners that year included actor Robert Redford, playwright Edward Albee, and songwriter Stephen Sondheim.

In 2006, Sendak published *Mommy?*, his one and only pop-up book.

Chapter 5
BACK TO CHILDREN'S BOOKS

Sendak tackled both current issues and old rhymes with 1993's *We Are All in the Dumps with Jack and Guy*. The story features two different Mother Goose rhymes. Sendak puts them together in an unusual way to tell the story of two homeless boys and an orphan baby. The baby is taken away by rats, and the two boys, Jack and Guy, work to get him back.

The illustrations for *We Are in the Dumps with Jack and Guy* add to the meaning of the story. The setting shows a modern-day city where children live in cardboard and wooden boxes. Newspaper headlines can be seen throughout the story, calling out about difficult times. In the book, *The Art of Maurice Sendak: 1980 to the Present*, Sendak explained that he had partly been inspired by something he saw while visiting Los Angeles once. He noticed "the naked feet of a kid sticking out of a cardboard box." That image helped him realize what "Jack and Guy could be: contemporary, political."

The cover illustration comes from a painting by Andrea Mantegna. The painting is called *The Descent Into Limbo* and it was made in the late 1400s. It shows a figure of Jesus Christ standing by the opening of a deep, dark cave. As he explained in a 2003 lecture, Sendak "copied the painting carefully and proudly" to use it as a symbol of "the terrifying world of lost children."

Still, even in this darkest of worlds, the children manage to survive. A large cat rescues Jack, Guy, the baby, and some kittens from the rats. The cat then changes into the moon, and whisks them all away from their earthly troubles for a while.

Sendak's next major project was a book adaptation of *Brundibár,* a famous children's opera. He teamed up with playwright Tony Kushner, who worked on the text for the 2003 book while Sendak did the illustrations.

THE STORY BEHIND BRUNDIBÁR

Brundibár was created by Adolf Hoffmeister and Hans Krása. Krása was a Czech composer who died during World War II. He was one of the millions of Jews sent to concentration camps by the Germans. Krása was imprisoned at a camp called Terezin for a time. At this camp, a group of children performed *Brundibár* fifty-five times. It was surprising that they were allowed to, since *Brundibár* is all about children joining together to get rid of a bully. Sadly, both *Brundibár's* composer and most of the children were put to death at another concentration camp.

Writer Tony Kushner and Sendak became good friends while working on Brundibár together.

In 2006, Sendak made a different type of book. He worked with Arthur Yorinks and Matthew Reinhart on his first and only pop-up book, *Mommy?* The reader follows along a child's search for his mother through a house filled with monsters. Using the pop-up book style, Sendak and his collaborators are able to surprise the reader with each turn of the page and the lifting of each flap.

No matter the project, Sendak created most of his later works at his home in Ridgefield. He liked to listen to music when he drew or painted. One of his most important musical influences was Mozart. He was also fond of the works of composer Giuseppe Verdi. In his later years, Sendak saw Verdi as an inspiration. Verdi wrote several of his best operas when he was in his eighties.

Sendak was influenced by a number of other artists and illustrators. Some of his work looks as if they may have come from a different place and time. This may be because Sendak admired so many artists from the past, such as Thomas Rowlandson and George Cruikshank. Rowlandson painted and made illustrations of English life during the 1700s and early 1800s. Cruikshank, another Englishman, created political cartoons and illustrations for children's books in the 1800s. In his Caldecott award acceptance speech, Sendak explained that he borrowed some of his techniques from these two artists.

Some have also commented on the European feel of Sendak's artwork. He found some inspiration in the works of French artist Louis-Maurice Boutet de Monvel and German artist

Wilhelm Busch. Boutet de Monvel painted watercolors and drew illustrations for children's books in the 1800s. Known for his comic images, Busch was the creator of *Max und Moritz*. Busch's influence on Sendak's style is clear in books such as *In the Night Kitchen*.

When he was writing, Sendak preferred quiet. But he liked to listen to classical music when he was drawing. In his different workspaces at home, he surrounded himself with many special items, including original artwork by the poet William Blake. Blake's art and poetry had a huge impact on Sendak, especially *Songs of Innocence and Experience*.

Sendak had a tremendous collection of books. A first edition copy of Herman Melville's *Moby Dick* was among his prized possessions. He also had a walking stick that once belonged to children's author Beatrix Potter. At the lectures and other appearances, Sendak would usually bring that cane along with him.

For much of his life, Sendak suffered from insomnia. This meant he didn't get much sleep. During the day, he always took a break in the afternoon. He liked to take long walks in the woods with his dogs. He even had a German shepherd called Herman, named for one of Sendak's favorite authors, Herman Melville.

Throughout his career, Sendak was incredibly generous with his readers. He answered countless letters from young fans. Over the years, Sendak also helped and encouraged numerous other writers and artists. Arthur Yorinks was just one of the talents

Sendak supported. Yorinks first entered in Sendak's life as a teenager. He appeared on the doorstep of Sendak's New York City apartment. Sendak and Yorinks eventually ended up collaborating on several projects.

No matter how busy he was, Sendak always made time to support other writers and artists and to communicate with fans.

Sendak joined Spike Jonze and actor Max Records for the movie premiere of *Where the Wild Things Are* in 2009 in New York City.

Chapter 6
FINAL YEARS

Sendak helped bring the wild things to life for the 2009 movie, *Where the Wild Things Are*. After some reluctance, he worked with director Spike Jonze on making a movie version of his most famous story. Sendak explained to the *Los Angeles Times* that he and Jonze made a good team. "With Spike, I found a genuine, fierce little artist."

As for the final film, Sendak seemed equally pleased: "It's not cute and cuddly! It's a real movie." The movie is moody and dark, much like Sendak's original picture book. Max is as lonely and angry a child as he was in the book. However, in the movie, he has an older teenage sister and a single mother who is clearly overworked. In this version, Max runs out of the house after a fight with his mother. In the woods he discovers a boat and travels across the water to a strange land with even stranger creatures. In the film, the audience sees more of Max's family life and his adventures with the wild things—but just as in the original story, he finds his way back to the warmth and comfort of home in the end.

WILD THINGS ON THE BIG SCREEN

The film version of *Where the Wild Things Are* was released in October 2009. In its first weekend in theaters, the film earned more than $32 million at the box office. Reviewers had mixed feelings about it, however. A writer for *Spin* magazine called it the "best heartbreaking adventure" of the year. Some critics didn't like the fact that the monsters talked, something they didn't do in the original story. By giving them words, the wild things became less scary. As a *Daily Variety* reporter said, "one never fears that any of them would dream of making a meal out of Max."

Jonze and his collaborator Lance Bangs also made a documentary about Sendak. They began working on the project in 2003. *Tell Them Anything You Want: A Portrait of Maurice Sendak* (2009) shows interviews done with Sendak at his Connecticut home. Sendak was around 80 years old when the documentary was made. He spoke a lot about those whom he had lost and his own eventual death. Still, the great writer-illustrator seemed excited about working on more books. He only complained that "the only thing wrong with being old is there is no time."

Two years later, Sendak published *Bumble-Ardy*, the first book that he both wrote and illustrated in thirty years. It was inspired by a short animated film that he had made for the television show Sesame Street in the 1970s. With its bold, comic style, Bumble-Ardy follows a nine-year-old pig on his quest to finally have a birthday party. His parents are dead, and he lives with his aunt Adeline. His aunt forbids him from throwing a party, but he has one anyway. She comes home to discover the party and sends the revelers away. While she's mad at first, Adeline forgives Bumble.

On the outside, the story looks like a happy tale. Sendak, however, viewed his main character as "a troubled pig-boy." As he told *The Horn Book Magazine*, Bumble-Ardy is "a lonely, unhappy kid who is doing the best he can to be in the world." For Sendak personally, the book helped him get through a terrible time. Dr. Eugene Glynn, his partner of fifty years, was dying of cancer. Glynn passed away in 2007. After Glynn's death, Sendak found working on *Bumble-Ardy* as a way to deal with his grief. He explained on the radio program *Fresh Air* that "When I did *Bumble-Ardy*, I was so intensely aware of death… I did Bumble-Ardy to save myself."

The year after *Bumble-Ardy*'s release, Sendak suffered a stroke. He was in a Danbury, Connecticut, hospital for several days before he passed away on May 7, 2012. He was eighty-three years old. His death made headlines around the globe. *The New York Times* heralded him as "A conjurer of luminous worlds, both beautiful and terrifying." Friends and fans alike mourned the loss of such a unique and enduring talent.

The world got one more Sendak original after his death. In 2013, his final project hit bookstore shelves. He had made *My Brother's Book* as a tribute to his brother Jack, who had died in 1995. In an interview with *The New Yorker* magazine, he explained that he "wanted to do something extraordinary" for Jack. Sendak had completed the book and had even seen final page proofs of *My Brother's Book* before his death.

For more than sixty years, Sendak shared his creative visions—in pictures and in words. He illustrated close to 100 books during his career. While the number of books he both wrote and illustrated was smaller, the impact of these stories has been tremendous. *Where the Wild Things Are* has become a lasting piece of our culture. Generations and generations of readers have accompanied Max on his journey. Like Sendak himself, the book remains popular because it is both true and fanciful.

As he explained in *Tell Them Anything You Want*, "I think what I've offered is different, but not because I drew better than anybody or wrote better than anybody. But because I was more honest than anybody."

SELECTED BOOKS WRITTEN AND ILLUSTRATED BY MAURICE SENDAK

Kenny's Window (Harper and Brothers, 1956)

The Sign on Rosie's Door (Harper and Brothers, 1960)

The Nutshell Library (Harper & Row, 1962)

Where the Wild Things Are (Harper & Row, 1963)

Higglety Pigglety Pop! or *There Must Be More to Life*
      (Harper & Row, 1967)

In the Night Kitchen (Harper & Row, 1970)

Ten Little Rabbits: A Counting Book with Mino the Magician
      (Rochenbach Foundation, 1970)

Some Swell Pup or Are You Sure You Want a Dog?
      (with Matthew Margolis, Farrar, Straus and Giroux, 1976)

Seven Little Monsters (Harper & Row, 1977)

Fantasy Sketches (Rochenbach Museum, 1981)

Outside Over There (Harper & Row, 1981)

Caldecott & Co: Notes on Books and Pictures
      (Michael di Capua Books, 1988)

We Are All in the Dumps with Jack and Guy (HarperCollins, 1993)

Bumble-Ardy (Michael di Capua Books, 2011)

SELECTED BOOKS ILLUSTRATED BY MAURICE SENDAK

During his long career, Sendak worked with many other children's authors. Here is just a sampling of some of the writers and books that were important to him.

A Hole Is to Dig (with Ruth Krauss)

Brundibar (with Tony Kushner)

Swine Lake (with James Marshall)

I Saw Esau (with Iona and Peter Opie)

Circus Girl (with Jack Sendak)

The Juniper Tree (with Lore Segal)

Mommy? (with Arthur Yorinks and Matthew Reinhart)

GLOSSARY

baptism—a person's initiation into a difficult role

collaborate—to work closely with someone on a project

debut—the first public appearance of a new product or publication

documentary—a film that covers real events or people

editor—the person in charge of a book's or other text's content and publication

Great Depression—the period of severe economic hardship in the United States beginning with the stock market crash in 1929 and ending in 1939

insomnia—a condition of being unable to get enough sleep

libretto—the words of an opera

Old Country—a term used to describe the native country of a person who has emigrated. For many Jewish immigrants like Sendak's family, the "Old Country" meant Poland.

persecution—hostility and sometimes violence directed at a person, especially because of political or religious beliefs

stroke—a "brain attack," or when the flow of oxygen to the brain is interrupted

trilogy—a set of three books meant to be read in order

CHRONOLOGY

June 10, 1928: Maurice Sendak is born in Brooklyn, New York.

1964: Sendak wins the Caldecott Medal for *Where the Wild Things Are*.

1970: Sendak receives the Hans Christian Andersen International Medal.

1982: *Outside Over There* wins the National Book Award.

1983: Sendak earns the Laura Ingalls Wilder Award.

1996: President Bill Clinton awards Sendak the National Medal of Arts.

2006: Sendak wins the first Astrid Lindgren Memorial Award. He shares the prize with Austrian writer Christine Noestlinger.

2007: His longtime partner, Dr. Eugene Glynn, dies.

2009: Spike Jonze's film version of *Where the Wild Things Are* is released.

May 8, 2012: Sendak dies in a hospital in Danbury, Connecticut.

FURTHER INFORMATION

Books

Gaines, Ann. *Maurice Sendak*. Hockessin, DE: Mitchell Lane Publishers, 2001.

Pascal, Janet B. *Who Was Maurice Sendak?* New York, NY: Penguin Group, 2013.

Websites

Sendak's publisher, HarperCollins, hosts a site which features more information:
www.harpercollins.com/authors/12708/Maurice_Sendak/index.aspx

The Maurice Sendak Collection at the Rosenbach Museum and Library:
www.rosenbach.org/learn/collections/maurice-sendak-collection

BIBLIOGRAPHY

BOOKS

Kushner, Tony. *The Art of Maurice Sendak: 1980 to the Present.* New York, NY: Harry N. Abrams Inc., 2003.

Lanes, Selma G. *The Art of Maurice Sendak.* New York, NY: Harry N. Abrams Inc., 1980.

Maguire, Gregory. *Making Mischief: A Maurice Sendak Appreciation.* New York, NY: William Morrow and Company, 2009.

Marcus, Leonard S., ed. *Dear Genius: The Letters of Ursula Nordstrom.* New York, NY. HarperCollins Publishers, 1998.

Sendak, Maurice. *Caldecott & Co: Notes on Books & Pictures.* Michael Di Capua Books. New York, NY: Farrar, Straus and Giroux, 1988.

Sendak, Philip. *In Grandpa's House.* New York, NY: Harper & Row, 1985.

PRINT ARTICLES

Cook, Marianna. "Wild Things." *New Yorker*, May 21, 2012.

Nelson, Valerie J. "Maurice Sendak, 1928-2012." *Los Angeles Times,* May 9, 2012.

Sendak, Maurice. "Descent into Limbo." *Children and Libraries,* Summer-Fall 2003.

Sendak, Maurice. "Ruth Krauss and Me: A Special Partnership." *Horn Book Magazine*, May-June 1993.

Sutton, Roger. "An Interview with Maurice Sendak." *Horn Book Magazine*, November-December 2003.

Zarin, Cynthia. "Maurice Sendak and the Perils of Childhood." *New Yorker*, April 17, 2006.

ONLINE SOURCES

"Fresh Air Remembers Maurice Sendak," National Public Radio www.npr.org/2012/05/08/152248901/fresh-air-remembers-author-maurice-sendak

"Maurice Sendak," Public Broadcasting System www.pbs.org/wnet/americanmasters/episodes/maurice-sendak/about-maurice-sendak/701

"Maurice Sendak Biography and Timeline," Rosenbach www.rosenbach.org/maurice-sendak-biography-and-timeline

"V.F. Portrait: Maurice Sendak," Vanity Fair www.vanityfair.com/culture/features/2011/08/maurice-sendak-201108

INDEX

ABOUT THE AUTHOR:

Wendy Mead spends much of her time writing about other people's lives. She has written several biographies, including *Sharon Creech* for the *Spotlight On Children's Authors* series. Wendy lives in Connecticut with her book-loving family.